MW00927987

The Nonprofit Leader Of The New Decade

By Jeffrey R. Wilcox, CFRE

—■■—

Copyright © 2010 Jeffrey R. Wilcox, CFRE

All rights reserved. No portion of this book may
be reproduced, stored in a retrieval system, or
transmitted in any form or by any means –
electronic, mechanical, photocopy, recording
or any other – except for brief quotations in printed
reviews, without prior written permission of the publishers.

Taking Nonprofit Organizations to Higher Ground In Their Service to Others®

Published by Third Sector Publishing
A Division of Executive Consulting for the Nonprofit Sector, Inc.
110 West Ocean Boulevard, Suite 340, Long Beach, CA 90802
and the
Long Beach Business Journal
A Division of South Coast Publishing, Inc.
2599 E. 28th Street, Suite 212, Signal Hill, CA 90755

ISBN 978-0-557-57336-3

Second Edition

Printed in the United States of America

In memory of my father,
Bill Wilcox

A master of community journalism
and a model of community leadership

ABOUT THIRD SECTOR REPORT
Committed To Fostering A Continuity of Leadership For The Nonprofit Sectors of the United States and Canada.

The Third Sector Report is the result of a partnership between The Long Beach Business Journal in Long Beach, California, and our firm, whose mission is to foster a continuity of leadership for the nonprofit sectors of the United States and Canada.

The introduction of our regular column in 2008 represented a deliberate and highly visible choice to demonstrate and fulfill our mission in a unique way: Engage business leaders on the fundamentals of community leadership.

The eight-part series, "The Nonprofit Leader of the New Decade," generated a tremendous following by corporate, association, nonprofit, governmental and community leaders. Readers indicated that each were at different places in thinking through the root causes of some of their organizational challenges.

This book, the first in a series, presents the content of the columns and offers a way for readers to engage in topical discussions about the highly unique aspects and attributes of being a leader in The Third Sector – in the past, in the present, and in the future.

I personally thank you for picking up a copy of our book and for joining a growing community of readers who have engaged with the contents of these columns to help their organizations to find higher ground in their service to others.

A big thanks to George Economides, founder and publisher of the Long Beach Business Journal, for being one of the first media professionals to endorse and recognize commentary about the nonprofit sector as an essential component of contemporary business journalism.

Sincerely,

JEFFREY R. WILCOX, CFRE
Columnist, Third Sector Report
The Long Beach Business Journal

Table of Contents

An Introduction
The Nonprofit Leader Of The New Decade

Nonprofit leaders of the new decade must recognize that the bottom line of their efforts has less to do with leadership and everything to do with legacy – what the next generation will inherit to continue advancing communities as a result of their leadership.

Leadership. It's one of those words that virtually every businessperson uses at least once a day. And yet, depending on the context, the word has significantly different meanings for different people.

Business leadership, political leadership, team leadership and community leadership are but a few of the different cachets the word attracts. Fortunately, most wise leaders know that leadership proficiency in one context doesn't always equate to success in another.

At the dawn of the second decade of the twenty-first century – weathering economic turmoil unsurpassed in prior decades – leaders of community-based nonprofit organizations across the continent are being forced to take a sobering look at the lessons learned from leading community organizations over the past decades in order to thoughtfully chart for the next one.

In order to bridge the sector's past with its future, we must agree that there are leadership attributes, to quote Jim Collins in his monograph, "Good To Great For The Social Sector," that separate those persons who provide good community leadership from those who will be known for providing great leadership to the entire nonprofit sector.

In summary format, here are those leadership attributes that I believe separates the former leader from the latter. It is, in fact, how the leader demonstrates these attributes that a legacy will emerge for the next generation to inherit and to lead organizations to higher ground in their service to others during the next ten years:

#1
Nonprofit leaders of the new decade must see themselves as leading causes not organizations.

"Our organization was a cause before it ever become an organization" should be often said reminder to all followers of a great nonprofit leader.

The nonprofit organization is the result of a growing number of people who champion a cause that eventually needs an infrastructure to support them. In essence, a great cause with great leadership births a great organization.

Savvy nonprofit leaders approach their craft and grow their organization by applying the same formula. Knowing what comes first and keeping that first puts the organization in its rightful place within the framework of a cause – standing behind people who want to make a difference – not above them and not in front of them.

#2
Savvy nonprofit leaders must know the difference between values and virtues.

When a leader views the nonprofit as an organized community of people with a cause, the leader understands that upholding a clearly articulated and widely distributed set of values is job number one.

These values, held by the community, articulate what the organization stands for in bettering society. Compelling values that state "what we believe" serve as a guide for shaping people's work, the organization's decisions, and the leader's conscience.

There are three critical reasons for nonprofit leaders to take values seriously. First, the mission statement has no foundation in which it can stand without a base of values to which it finds its meaning. Second, people who are impassioned and empowered by a set of values have lower rates of attrition. And third, research proves overwhelmingly that it is the organization's values that, ultimately, are the deciding factor for people who are considering significant and sustaining financial contributions.

Beware the nonprofit that believes it must tell the world that accountability is one of their "values statements," joining other things like honesty, integrity or open communication. Contributors to a cause should expect any self-respecting charitable organization to embrace virtues that value integrity.

Striving to be a virtuous organization does not equate to being a valuable cause to a community worthy of support.

#3
Nonprofit leaders must take calculated risks to keep pace with society.

The "Achilles' Heel" for The Third Sector is the statement:
"We've always done it this way!"

The fact is social entrepreneurs are the ones who spawned great and resilient organizations of the nonprofit sector. The founders of these organizations may have passed on, but that doesn't mean that the entrepreneurial spirit that built these organizations has been put to rest.

The successful nonprofit in the new decade is led by people who encourage, engage, and recognize pioneering approaches to shaping services, involving people in their cause, and masterminding resilient and dynamic organizations to support.

The nonprofit leader of the new decade must push the envelope for participatory, virtual, non-bureaucratic and non-hierarchical approaches to evolving communities.

#4
Sector leaders must demonstrate that human capital is a more significant contributor to a nonprofit's equity than financial capital.

The mantra is simple: *"Put people first, not their dollars."* This has been the formula for the founders of most successful nonprofit organizations.

Fortunately for us, these individuals did not wait for sufficient financial capital to start their causes. If they had, the list of nonprofit organizations today would be shockingly small, and the amount of need in local communities would be massive.

Today, however, there is clear evidence of a rapidly shrinking percentage of sector leaders who are unwilling to acknowledge the mantra of putting people first. Further concern is that these leaders are not willing to take what is viewed as a large financial risk to at least test the mantra for it to prove itself once again.

For the contemporary leader, as well as for his or her predecessors of decades ago, the fundraising formula begins by counting total numbers of contributors first and their financial contributions second. The sustainable nonprofit has a large base of human capital from which to evolve their financial capital in good times and bad.

Beware the leader who narrowly defines the nonprofit's "workforce" as the paid employees. It devalues the sweat equity that got a nonprofit started and it stops the organization's evolution.

#5
Contemporary nonprofit leaders must view governance as a dynamic organization development process.

A dynamic board of directors of a nonprofit sits at the center of the organization, not atop the organization as though it was a corporation.

Something really goes wrong in the sector when a group of people decides they could or should move to a position of being over people instead of moving to a place of growing the number of people surrounding them.

The strength of governance lies not in pulling people and their contributions up through a hierarchy, but rather in its ability to draw people and their contributions closer to the center of leading a viable, lawful, orderly, accountable and sound cause.

Words like "ad hoc, task force, project team, and work group" are the vocabulary used by nonprofit leaders of the new decade as they gather information and stimulate ideas that reflect innovative and contemporary policy-making with fiduciary due diligence.

With a growing number of Gen X and Ys who want to be a part of the community, "sitting" on boards and committees to populate a hierarchy isn't going to create an avalanche of accepted invitations. "Being in the center of it all," offers a much different appeal for people driven to help others.

#6
As financial managers, the pioneering leader must challenge old definitions and out-dated formulas in order to redefine what stewardship means in the new decade.

A new expression in nonprofit nomenclature is "The Starvation Cycle," which says that unless our leaders come up with a new way of redefining overhead and measuring ROI (return on investment), the sector is destined to starve itself to demise.

Sector leaders must be willing to wave the red flag to stop using measures that were borrowed and applied from other industries as though they are the standards for this one.

The new decade leader is hungry to pioneer a set of metrics and measures of success that are unique to the nonprofit industry, while sufficiently proving ethical stewardship, organizational viability, and solid returns on people's investments of time, knowledge, and money to make the world a better place.

The time is right to re-define what stewardship means in the twenty-first century and we've got a new generation of innovators who are able to figure that out in their own terms, and should be given the opportunity to do so sooner than later.

#7

Revitalizing the practice of advocacy is a mandate that must capture and hold the leader's enthusiastic attention if we are to capture and hold the attention of the next generation.

It is the convening of people and the rallying for their support that turns a few good citizens with a cause into a nonprofit organization. The nonprofit leader of the new decade must be focused on "public engagement" not "public education" as the key to growth in both contributors and their contributions.

If the first decade of this century is any indication, ways to engage people are going to have more platforms and venues to bring more people together behind great causes than ever before. The next–generation leader to the sector must consider that a legacy of being "the great convener" has an impact on the organization that is significantly more far-reaching than the leader striving to be the "the great communicator."

As we enter this new decade, I see countless organizations stuck between what they were, what they are and what they want to be in the future. Today we have more ways to bring about a reconciliation than ever before.

The nonprofit leader of the new decade realizes that helping people to reconcile an organization's past with its future is the single greatest contribution to the long-term viability and impact of the cause that the organization is in business to support.

The sobering truth about nonprofit leadership in the new decade: It's not about leading change …It's about facilitating evolution.

That's a different kind of leader. And, that's a different skill set than our colleagues from the other sectors generally bring with them to leadership positions in the nonprofit sector.

The seven leadership directives outlined in this book are offered as tools to help new decade nonprofit leaders to first contemplate the task of evolving a cause, and then to be in meaningful dialogue with others to get the job done. Along the way, good leadership requires thoughtful dialogue with people that will result in evolving decisions about building and sustaining human and financial capital, policy-based governance, risk-taking decision-making, and values-based accountability.

Whether my colleagues agree with these attributes or not, we must all agree that those of us who call ourselves leaders need to be modeling, more so now than ever before, to the next generation, what it means and what it looks like to be a great community leader. Or, stated in a way that I think Jim Collins would encourage, the nonprofit leader of the new decade must be demonstrating excellent examples of legislative leadership in action for the next generation to emulate before it's too late and the practice becomes extinct.

Indeed, I believe there was a unique leadership legacy that separated the evolving nonprofit organization when the founders moved on from the eroding organization that died soon after its founders. My intent is to better understand the legacy that I inherited as a nonprofit leader and to invite scores of other leaders and readers to join with me to craft a legacy that will hold the same promise for the next generation of leaders so they, too, step into leadership positions believing they have the ability to shape society, change people's lives, and evolve a nation.

Succession planning begins with our entire sector if we have any hope for succession to occur in our favorite organizations.

What, then, is the call of the Nonprofit Leader of the New Decade?

My Response:
Leaving A Legacy For How To Effectively Lead People and Organizations Such That The Next Generation Can Advance Their Communities And Successfully Usher Society Into The Post Baby Boomer Era

My fear is that if community leaders don't accept this challenge at the dawn of the new decade, the viability of the nonprofit sector as a whole will be threatened by the end of the decade.

An Assessment:
Viewing Leadership Through A "Next Decade" Lens

For each of the variables identified in "The Nonprofit Leader of the New Decade," assign a rating, on a scale of one to four, for the level of importance you perceive each of these factors to be in successfully leading nonprofit organizations and the people that work for, support and benefit from their work.

Additionally, for each leadership factor, assign a rating of how evident this factor is in your leadership of a nonprofit organization.

A rating of "1" represents the lowest score and a rating of "4" represents the highest score. There is no middle of the road score when it comes to leadership.

The Nonprofit Leader of the New Decade variables:

1. Leads a "cause" versus an "organization"

How Important Do You Think This Is?	1	2	3	4
How Evident Is This In Your Leadership?	1	2	3	4

2. Leads according to "values" versus "virtues"

How Important Do You Think This Is?	1	2	3	4
How Evident Is This In Your Leadership?	1	2	3	4

3. Takes calculated risks to serve others

How Important Do You Think This Is?	1	2	3	4
How Evident Is This In Your Leadership?	1	2	3	4

4. Embraces human capital as the highest form of equity for organizational sustainability

How Important Do You Think This Is?	1	2	3	4
How Evident Is This In Your Leadership?	1	2	3	4

5. Practices dynamic governance

How Important Do You Think This Is?	1	2	3	4
How Evident Is This In Your Leadership?	1	2	3	4

6. **Pioneers new metrics and formulas to fairly evaluate organizational and leadership success**

How Important Do You Think This Is?	1	2	3	4
How Evident Is This In Your Leadership?	1	2	3	4

7. **Embraces advocacy as an essential strategy for the organization's sustainability**

How Important Do You Think This Is?	1	2	3	4
How Evident Is This In Your Leadership?	1	2	3	4

Your observations and thoughts about which of these attributes are most applicable to the leadership needs of your nonprofit organization.

_____

_____

_____

What specific "first steps" will you take to evolve your facilitative leadership style to evolve as a community?

_____

_____

_____

_____

_____

_____

_____

What are the reactions of others to their scores?

_____

_____

_____

_____

_____

_____

_____

_____

Additional notes:

_____

_____

_____

_____

_____

_____

_____

_____

—1—

What Is The Nonprofit Leader Really Leading?

If a nonprofit leader thinks that what is being led is a corporation with a special tax classification, the people who stand behind, work for, and contribute to that organization are more than likely hoping their leader gets a different idea sooner than later.

In 2005, famed business author Jim Collins rocked The Third Sector with the publishing of his monograph, "Good to Great for the Social Sector." What is most astonishing about this adjunct piece to his book, "Good to Great," is its sub-title: Why business thinking is not the answer.

For most of my career, I, and many of my colleagues, have had to live with the widely held perception within the private sector that what the nonprofit sector really needs, is a big dose of business leadership to get it right.

Shortly after the booklet was published, Collins stated, "Working on the monograph taught me that there are significant differences between the business and the social sectors. The inputs, outputs and measurements of greatness are not the same."

Perhaps the most profound and lasting contribution Jim Collins provides to The Third Sector is his argument that business relies on "executive leadership" to achieve greatness, while the nonprofit leader exercises "legislative leadership."

What that basically says to me is that a chief executive officer doesn't automatically make for a good senator.

If the senator treats his constituents as though he or she is their chief executive standing over people as opposed to having surrounded himself or herself with people to earn their respect to act on their behalf, the chances for attracting followers, contributors and contributions are significantly reduced.

I further translate Collin's concept to mean there is a significant difference between the leader "in control" versus the leader "in command."

Unlike the business leader, the nonprofit leader recognizes that "what" is leading the organization is the ultimate question for success, not "who" is leading the organization.

In order for a nonprofit to exist, there is a driving force that fuels sweat equity, contributions of time and knowledge and passion. It is, indeed, a "what."

Whether it's to find a cure for diseases like polio, cancer or arthritis, or to assure that children grow up healthy and safe, the "what" is the cause.

Third Sector leaders desiring a legacy see themselves as leading causes not organizations.

Somewhere along the line, nonprofit leaders can get into trouble when their attention turns from the cause. There will be a natural disharmony created between leaders and their followers when perceptions of the driving forces behind the nonprofit are different.

Nonprofit leaders must always remember that it is people with a passion for a cause that births an organization. The flame that ignites the spark is human capital, not financial capital, and it remains the greatest source of capital for a nonprofit's future as we look towards the decade ahead.

The nonprofit leaders of the new decade are inheriting organizations that are being choked by the corporate model of leadership.

Fundraising, for example, is becoming such a sales management model that the importance of facilitating community "buy-in" is being lost. A fundamental prerequisite of leadership in fundraising is that people will "cash-in" if given a chance to "buy in" to the cause.

Today, we have boards of directors who see themselves as serving above people, like in a company, rather than leaders at the center of the organization who are surrounded by people.

Leadership in a nonprofit is a hub-and-spoke system of human capital at work for a cause.

Here's one example among many to prove the point of what is meant by a nonprofit led as a cause not as a corporation:

Several years ago, a faith-based community created a home for the aging so that elderly members had a place to live and to receive quality care in their golden years. Once the home was constructed and operating, the board of directors evolved into a corporate-style board, with every moment spent overseeing a home.

Over time, the board began seeing indicators of trouble: Fundraising numbers were declining; census was dropping; waiting lists were no longer needed; and marketing efforts were all about mass appeals.

When the board was challenged to identify "what" motivated people in the community to come together, in the first place, to build a home, things began to change.

These leaders came to the realization that the building of the home was the result of a deeply held and shared community value: Honoring thy mother and thy father.

Perhaps the substantial contributions required to open the facility were less about covering capital costs and more about investing in a shared set of values we'll call "a cause."

Why did the efforts to get the whole community involved with honoring parents as a significant community cause stop when the building was built?

In this instance, a group of overseers of a corporation were soon transformed into a group of community leaders responsible for rebuilding a community surrounding a cause. The home was merely one manifestation of the cause. There was more work to be done and many new opportunities to pursue as people wanted to exercise many options in caring for their parents.

Thanks to their leadership, what followed was a series of community forums about the needs of families today. A series of new service programs were developed, and a flood of new ideas for helping a community to embrace, support and serve a new generation of older community members were invited.

People became involved. Not in a home, but in a cause ... the same cause that spawned the building of the home in the first place. Contributions and contributors soon followed because of the rallying effect these leaders and this organization had on a common and deeply held value.

"It was not a matter of recasting our work, it was matter of recasting our leadership," admits the chair of the board.

Corporate leadership and community leadership are two distinctly different kinds of leadership.

Over the years, I have had the opportunity to work with many nonprofit organizations that have struggled to keep their institutions viable. Unfortunately, despite all of their business efforts, a turnaround was not taking place. When we turned the conversation from leading an organization into leading a cause, however, the turnaround began.

Jim Collins makes a point in his monograph that the right people in nonprofit leadership understand that they do not have "jobs" as in business, but, rather, they have "responsibilities." In terms of what Collins suggests, as illustrated in this example, the leadership job may be governance of a care facility, but the responsibility is rallying a community behind the kind of care that all elders deserve and, then, leading the community to seeing and making that happen. The entire process became a demonstration of a community honoring its elders with human and financial capital to continue the cause into the next generation.

So, what, then, is the nonprofit leader really leading? The answer is people who share a passion for a common cause.

The community leader sees him or her as a leader of people not an organization. Without impassioned people, there is no organization over which to preside. Without impassioned people, there is no life-long contributing relationship to the organization.

The nonprofit leaders who move causes from good to great know that the leadership of a great senator comes first, and the leadership of a great chief executive, who assures a strong organization is standing behind the cause, must always come second.

Theory Into Practice:
The Nonprofit Leader of the New Decade

If a board of directors of a nonprofit care facility for the aged can transform their organization into a cause for demonstrating a community's shared commitment to honoring the mothers and fathers of the community; *and*

If a board of directors of a nonprofit botanical garden in an ethnic area of major city can transform their organization into a cause for sustaining a living tribute to the immigration and history of the people that established that neighborhood; *and*

If a board of directors launches an unsuccessful capital campaign for a neighborhood center and realizes that the cause is not building a building, but rather the revitalization of a neighborhood ...

**What, then, is the real cause the nonprofit organization
that you are leading represent to others?**

_____

_____

_____

_____

_____

_____

_____

_____

_____

_____

—2—

Creating and Sustaining The Passion For The Cause

**"What does the organization stand for?"
is not a multiple-choice question for the
nonprofit leader.**

The holidays are a time for many people to reflect on those things that mean the most to them. There is almost a sense of magic in the air as people connect with their families, send good wishes to others, sing familiar songs, and reflect on their personal faith.

It's almost uncanny what happens to people and those around them when these familiar and joyful activities are shared. Even Ebenezer Scrooge is able to catch the spirit of the season because of the contagious ways people celebrate and share their values.

The top finding in a study about charitable giving, conducted by the Association of Fundraising Professionals, is the high importance that contributors place on the values of the organization. People give to organizations whose values most closely align with their own.

Despite the findings, the numbers of nonprofit organizations that actually operate from a stated set of values are very few. Somewhere along the line, nonprofit board members and executives began to confuse the values of the organization with its virtues. There is a big difference between the two concepts.

The Passion For An Organization
Is Fueled By Values That Mobilize Not Describe

Virtues speak to such things as transparency, honest dealings, and integrity in the use of contributed dollars, and treating people with dignity. One hopes that every single nonprofit organization, regardless of the service it provides to the community, openly practices the virtues of a trustworthy and law-abiding professional charity.

In my experience, what has generally been referred to as "values statements," are, in actuality, standards of conduct or Codes of Ethics. Every good organization annually discusses, publishes, and adheres to a set of professional behaviors.

Great nonprofit leaders are aware that virtues do not generate passion. They create order, public confidence, and trust. Stating a commitment to honesty, open communications, fair treatment, or partnering with other organizations is not the fuel that energizes people to get involved, to stay involved, to contribute and to publicly defend an organization when the chips are down.

The virtues of a worthy cause
are not its values in society.

Values put a stake in the ground about the bond that holds people together behind a cause. A mission statement is the sum of what the world will look like by people demonstrating and contributing to these values. Beware the nonprofit that believes it needs both a mission and vision. What it really needs is a set of values with a visionary mission statement.

There is a distinct difference in the leadership qualities between people who lead organizations and people who lead causes. The development, demonstration, and advocacy for a stated set of values take center stage as the fundamental difference.
In essence, a statement of organizational values reads much like a creed. It says, "This is what we believe." Even the shortest history

lessons in nonprofit organizations will tell anyone of The Third Sector's religious roots. The idea of having missions is the clearest indicator; and, in a sense, the people who subscribe to missions are, in practice, missionaries.

Let me give you a couple of examples of values developed by nonprofit organizations:

An animal welfare organization has the following values, among a longer list of tenets:

We believe ...

- animals have the right to be free from cruelty, neglect and abuse;
- in the importance of ending companion animal over-population;
- animals have the capability to express their natural and innate behaviors in appropriate ways; and
- companion animals deserve caring guardianship.

A theatrical arts organization lists the following values, among a statement of ten:

We believe ...

- we have a responsibility to contribute to the intellectual development of our community;
- the appreciation and practice of arts must occur in the community as often as in the performing arts hall;
- local creators and their artistic creations must be championed by the community and in the community; and
- arts organizations, at best, are non-hierarchical coop-eratives in service to the community and the craftsman

A veteran's organization might list a value such as this as part of defining their cause ...

We believe:

- returning veterans who have fought for our freedom are deserving of community services and support to aid in their reentry into society as independent and self-sufficient citizens

Of all the work that I have done to support nonprofit organizations in their evolution, the discussions and developmental processes that have lead to a statement of organizational values has, without a doubt, been the most transformational. They have also been the most rewarding for me.

It is as though the fundamental truth, founding principles or the raison d'être have all been found and recorded for everyone involved in the cause to understand, iterate, and celebrate.

Planning processes actually become easier. A vision for the future becomes much clearer. The reasons to give, to get involved, and to get excited become more clearly stated.

Many people become uncomfortable with the discussion of values and their practice. It is the surest sign of the nonprofit sector's religious roots. It does not take a rocket scientist to understand why the word "mission" is such a part of the nonprofit nomenclature and culture. The thought of people on a mission or acting as "missionaries" have been a part of creating and changing communities for thousands of years.

Regardless of the possible discomfort, one cannot deny that great causes all started with a group of people impassioned by the thought of changing the world. Creeds, oaths, statements of belief, anthems, and founding principles are all examples of stated words that act as a tie that binds people.

Great things have happened in communities because of the passions of people. To truly "unleash the power of us," the nonprofit leader of the new decade must make the time to firmly ground the organization – its leadership, staff, volunteers and contributors – on the guiding values.

In demonstrating these values through service to the community, an organization takes on significant value to more and more of its people. The result is growing equity for the organization thanks to the human and financial capital provided to see these values evolve.

Theory Into Practice:
The Nonprofit Leader of the New Decade

A veteran's organization decides to firmly establish a set of values that will transform their organization into a cause. They begin their discussion with ...

*We believe that every man and woman
who lives in this community and has served our country
is entitled to ...*

A children's health organization decides to establish a set of values that will transform their organization into a cause. They begin their discussion with ...

*The health of a child must be safeguarded
by the entire community. Therefore, we believe ...*

A nonprofit theatrical company decides to establish a set of values that will transform their organization into a cause. They begin their discussion with ...

The contributions of theatrical arts must advance the welfare and intellectual development of our entire community. Therefore, we believe ...

If you were to begin a discussion about what your organization stands for and its value to society, how would you begin the sentence and how would you facilitate a process to work in the community with others to complete the sentence?

We believe ...

_____

_____

_____

_____

_____

_____

—3—

Taking The Calculated Risk For Your Cause

If a nonprofit organization wants to contribute to and enhance society, it must first have leaders focused on keeping pace with society.

When is the last time you heard those immortal words, "But we've always done it this way," as the key reason to avoid a discussion that could result in a significant change?

For those causes that we believe in, volunteer for, and contribute to, the notion of change can be daunting. First, because it challenges tradition; second, because it evokes emotional reactions; and third, because it most certainly requires conversations, consensus building, and conflict resolution.

That's hard work, and for many of us, we're not looking for that in our community activities.

No matter your stance on the recent health care reform discussion, we all had a chance to see how difficult it is to change something that affects people and society.

The health care reform debate is an example of the difficult decision-making processes nonprofit organizations face on a regular basis.

The processes associated with wrestling with different ideas that propose and implement change for impacting people's lives are emotional, complicated, and, often, highly political with an economic implication.

The truth is, nonprofit organizations help people face these kinds of challenges all the time. Whenever an individual is confronted with change it can create varying levels of emotion.

The successful nonprofit leader over the next ten years has no choice but to take a calculated risk if their causes and the organizations that sustain them are to remain viable in an ever-changing community.

As Dr. Elisa Nicholas, Chief Executive Officer of The Children's Clinic – Serving Children and Their Families – in Long Beach, so aptly put it when she said: "It's a matter of knowing when to grow, when to slow and when to let go." And, Elisa ought to know based on her 22-year track record of success.

The Children's Clinic took a calculated risk as parents were turning to Elisa and her staff for information and help, not only for their children, but also for themselves and other family members. "We had to really take a good look at our cause. It was vital that we evolved our original view of a child in medical need into a holistic view of a healthy child living in a family and community context."

The Children's Clinic made some extremely difficult decisions to redefine and expand its services to assure that children were living in a healthy environment, which would include defined services to adults and family members. This was a difficult decision, but one that clearly represented a unique loyalty to the cause of children's health in our community.

Patrice Wong, Executive Director at Long Beach Day Nursery, began her position at a time when one of our community's longest-standing nonprofits was at the crossroads in its fiscal viability and long-term sustainability.

Risk means for leaders to weigh depth of service over breadth of service to a community.

Providing affordable day care for working parents is a challenge to not only all nonprofit organizations dedicated to the cause, but also to employers who recognize the financial and family impact of quality care while away from home and school. Long Beach Day Nursery, like so many other care providers, also found itself faced with a myriad of situations challenging the children in their care. There were health, financial, safety, and family conflict issues, among many others, that demanded attention.

"We made an incredibly difficult decision at a time when other similar organizations were expanding services," Patrice explains. "We decided to deepen our services to children rather than to broaden them."

For the Board of Long Beach Day Nursery, that meant reducing the number of children served as well as closing a service site. Some could say that decision flies in the face of need, but others, including me, would say that says something about loyalty to a cause.

Patrice explains the calculated risk best when she remarks, "We decided the stretch should occur in quality of care, not a stretch in slots of care."

This, too, was a painful decision, but the results of that decision has maintained an accreditation for Long Beach Day Nursery that is the highest in our nation for quality care. It paved the way for an organization that stands at the threshold of its centennial of service to our community.

The Board at Musical Theatre West knew that the cause of preserving a uniquely American art form would be challenged if growing audiences of Generation X and Generation Y theatre-goers were not part of the organization's sustainability planning. In 2009, Musical Theatre West opened with the production of "Rent," which symbolized the most significant departure from its typical seasons that have entertained and educated audiences for decades.

Founding Executive Director and Producer Paul Garman says that this was a significant risk and the center of lively discussion. The result: A business development decision that dramatically changed the demographic of the Musical Theatre West audience.

The biggest learning in this process, according to Lucy Daggett, Chairman of the Governance Committee, was the organization's need to change its evaluation criteria. "Using old criteria, some would say our risk wasn't worth it. Using new evaluation criteria, it was priceless."

Every nonprofit leader realizes that the idea of the "nimble organization" is a whole different ballgame when there are volunteers, community leaders, contributors and stakeholders involved. But, the nonprofit leader of the new decade reminds everyone that the great organizations serving our community are the result of a few people taking a huge risk because they believe so deeply in their cause. The future generation is expecting nothing less of us.

Theory Into Practice:
The Nonprofit Leader of the New Decade

The Children's Clinic made a conscious decision to evolve their mission to extend services to family members.

How would you lead a decision-making process to potentially re-interpret the mission of your organization based on your experiences you've gained in providing services to the community?

Long Beach Day Nursery made a conscious decision to move from serving more people to better serving less people.

How would you lead a decision-making process to consider the potential of serving fewer people but with higher quality services?

Musical Theatre West made a conscious decision to expand services to attract and sustain participation by Generation X and Generation Y.

How would you lead a decision-making process to take a calculated risk to effectively increase the sustainable numbers of Generation X and Generation Y people involved in your organization?

Theory Into Practice:
The Nonprofit Leader of the New Decade

**What are are two examples of risks
that your nonprofit organization has taken
over the past few years?**

_____

_____

_____

_____

**What lessons can current leadership
learn from these two examples
in directing future decision-making?**

_____

_____

_____

_____

**Are there are application of these lessons
to the decision-making processes of your organization?**

_____

_____

_____

_____

—4—

The Nonprofit Workforce Of The New Decade

The nonprofit leader must view human capital development as primary to financial capital development in building and sustaining a community's equity in an organization.

The U.S. Department of Labor released its findings in early 2010 about voluntarism in the United States, and the news is very heartening. Both the number of people volunteering and the amount of time these men and women of all ages are providing to local communities is rising.

The good news is that voluntarism, especially during these challenging times, remains very much a unique and edifying thread in the American tapestry.

Behind the good news, however, are two sets of numbers that can no longer go unnoticed by the nonprofit leader of the new decade. The first set of numbers is the rate of voluntarism among generations other than the Baby Boomers and their parents. The second statistic is that the number of people who are choosing nonprofit careers is falling far short of the vacancies that Baby Boomers are creating in The Third Sector as they retire.

The concept of workforce planning is becoming a popular trend in business. The concept is a systematic and fully integrated organizational process to proactively plan ahead to avoid talent surplus and talent shortage within the organization.

The nonprofit workforce is a unique combination of paid and unpaid human resources, and it is the only sector in our economy with such advantages. The practice of workforce planning in The Third Sector, therefore, is a different human resource science.

Colleen Kelly, Executive Director of Vantage Point and Volunteer Vancouver (BC) and author of "A People Lens," says that nonprofit workforce planning is about developing and deploying people who provide their "heads" and their "hands" for the benefit of the organization.

Colleen does not make the distinction of who are paid and who are unpaid.

In the new decade, nonprofit leaders must retire the notion that lack of staff resources is holding the organization back. The fact is, nonprofits will never, ever have enough staff resources to get the job done of building communities and helping people in need.

Workforce planning for the nonprofit sector calls for leaders to develop human capital for their organizations and at a level that is on par with their enthusiasm for raising financial capital for their causes.

The discomforting news for the Baby Boomers is that engaging people to work or volunteer for a nonprofit organization during the new decade is quite different from the approaches employed to engage and retain them.

An important term to know in the new decade is "Knowledge Philanthropist"

Colleen predicts that "knowledge philanthropists" are the next generation on the nonprofit landscape. It's a term she has coined that is spawning radical thinking about nonprofit workforce planning across both the United States and Canada.

In general, knowledge philanthropists want to invent, to re-engineer and to lead. They want to do something great and, often, independently on their own time and in their own home computer environment. They want to work with people they help select and they accomplish the work on terms they create. The notion of "sitting" on a board or on a committee is not attractive. Enlisting for three-year terms and adhering to conditions like "give or get" doesn't cut it.

One could make the argument we have a new generation of pioneers that mirror the kind of people who actually got today's nonprofit organizations off the ground.

Short, directed commitments and contributions with high involvement, clear accountability, visible recognition and social media communication is nonprofit management of the future.

The terms "work team, ad-hoc, and task force" are tools for planning paid and unpaid human resources to work in a less hierarchical structure. "Community expert, knowledge leader, community consultant and project coordinator" are terms used in lieu of "volunteer." The skills of "facilitator, coordinator, trainer, convener, and mediator" are the talents to be recruited and cultivated in the nonprofit leader whether paid or unpaid. The notion of "underpaid administrator" must yield to "social entrepreneur" if the sector is to draw the next generation of nonprofit professionals.

**The language of community leadership
is at the heart of the practice of community leadership.**

I had the opportunity to join with Colleen in challenging 15 executive directors of nonprofit organizations in Los Angeles to think through workforce planning for the new decade. Among the most common comments:

- "We can't view volunteers in that way"
- "We can't take those responsibilities away from the board"
- "There are certain things that staff must control" and
- "You can't hold volunteers that accountable."

I was reminded how uncomfortable some leaders were about a hundred years ago at the thought of women voting.

By the end of the discussion, every single nonprofit executive began to realize the silo effect that had overtaken their organizations because of some need to draw absolutes that differentiate between the paid workforces from the voluntary workforce. They realized how the hunger for human capital was being abandoned in the pursuit of financial capital. They also realized volunteer job descriptions were based on what the nonprofit wanted from the volunteer, not on what the volunteer could offer the organization.

They also realized the corporate structure in their organizations may have overtaken the community structures that actually created their founding and growth.

The harnessing and management of "knowledge philanthropy" is the challenge that lies ahead.

I can't wait to see what the future brings if the nonprofit leader of the new decade sees himself or herself as responsible for helping to unlock the human potential that is in our community to contribute back to our community.

Theory Into Practice:
The Nonprofit Leader of the New Decade

**Human capital forms a unique form
of equity for a sustainable nonprofit organization.**

*To what extent is the building of human capital building addressed in your
annual or strategic planning processes?*

_____

_____

_____

**Human capital is primary to financial capital
in building the sustainable nonprofit organization.**

*To what extent is the building of human capital addressed in your resource
development philosophy and practice?*

_____

_____

_____

**"Knowledge philanthropy" and "Social entrepreneur"
are terms that are gaining momentum in the sector.**

*To what extent is knowledge philanthropy and social entrepreneurship
addressed in your decision-making about the future?*

_____

_____

_____

—5—

Dynamic Governance of Nonprofits

**How a leader responds to the question,
"How Is This Organization Led?"
provides the telling answers about a leader's approach to
governance of a corporation versus governance of a cause.**

As we enter the new decade, the traditional model of how nonprofit organizations are governed is changing significantly. And there are good reasons for that.

The first reason has to do with a new generation of board members who are looking for different outcomes from their board experience than previous generations. Many of my colleagues are truly challenged by board recruitment and are commenting that the demographic profile of the type of person they are seeking for board positions is a shrinking percentage of the population.

What lured Baby Boomers to nonprofit boards is not what lures their successors.

The next generation nonprofit leader must acknowledge that those individuals willing to volunteer for multi-year commitments, sit through at least 30 meetings over a three-year period, adhere to "give or get" requirements, and agree to very specific tasks imposed on everyone are simply becoming fewer.

The second reason is the dynamic environment that all sectors of our community must operate within to remain vital, supported, and active. The ability to make fast decisions and impose quick changes in how things are done is a critical need for nonprofits as public funding sources make quick and radical decisions, social needs change, opportunities for partnership arise, and other organizations significantly modify their services or cease operations.

The nonprofit leader of the new decade must take a good look at the infrastructure of the cause each and every year. Period.

When a board approves a very clear picture of success with stated measurements, the next question is: "How can our organization of paid and unpaid human resources work together best to accomplish these very clear board-approved goals?"

Infrastructure change in a nonprofit is hard work and it's emotional. Disbanding a volunteer committee that has existed for a number of years is like asking a long-time employee to look at their position differently or to consider retirement. Position elimination, whether it affects an employee or a committed volunteer, requires the same leadership know-how.

The name of the game today is ad hoc, task force, and project teams. There is also a growing movement to classify some committees as "governance" committees that report directly to the board for policy-making and board development purposes. Other committees are designated as "operations" committees and report directly to the executive director and senior management to carry out tasks and strategies that reflect implementation of policy rather than creation of policy.

A nonprofit board doesn't sit atop the organization above people; rather, it sits at the center of the organization surrounded by people.

Key to any serious discussion about a more dynamic governance structure for a nonprofit organization is the topic of control. "How much control does a board of directors need to have once it has created policy which sets the goals, outcomes and boundaries for others to carry out?" promises to be an energetic conversation starter in any nonprofit organization that now must take place as we look ahead.

At the heart of this discussion, however, is a fundamental truth that separates these ideas from "making sense" and "making no sense" to the reader.

The nonprofit leader of the new decade must recognize that the voluntary community-based board of directors sits at the center of the organization and not atop the organization as though this was a corporation.

Somewhere along the line, once an organization had been founded, grounded and organized into an organization, the community-based governance piece mysteriously elevated itself above everything and everybody. A hierarchy, by nature, stands in the way of change. A concentric set of circles grows and expands.

The future is about engaging people … not enlisting people.

We Baby Boomers are going to have to accept the fact that Generation X and Generation Y community leaders prefer to assemble with their friends, business colleagues and other people to help them in doing something of significance rather than inherit an established group of people in an established hierarchy.

The nomenclature of the new governance model is moving towards use of "assignment" rather than use of "appointment" when recruiting.

Ad hoc groups allow the nonprofit leader to recruit people with specialized tasks and skills to make a significant contribution based on "doing" rather than based on "sitting." It also creates a more flexible environment for managing human resources for bringing people in as opportunities change.

Let me give you an example of this governance model at work. I recently worked with a traditional corporate-type board at a nonprofit organization that sat "above" the organization in its thinking and practice.

Following a conversation about the need to establish organizational values for the cause, the first thing the board did, out of habit, was to collectively sigh at the thought of having to find another three hours in their calendars to "do the job."

I told them to put their calendars away. You don't tell people what their values are going to be!

The board was directed to talk about the process the organization should use that would result in a set of draft values that would eventually be presented to them for approval. We'll call that "setting policy" regarding determination of values. An additional policy will be needed regarding adhering to the values and their use throughout the organization.

The board decided that the process should be convening the alumni or "old-timers" of the organization to discuss their motivations for first getting involved and then staying involved with the organization. They also agreed there was significant worth in discussing values with their "youth board" which had recently formed. Here they could learn why these younger people got involved. The board then realized that a conversation about values would create a terrific reason to convene their top contributors to ask why they support the organization so generously.

**Governance works best as a facilitator for the cause ...
not a dictator to the cause.**

Board members became quite enthusiastic about serving as "facilitators" of values rather than "dictators" of values. The number of people willing to volunteer to meet and be in dialogue with key stakeholders, and then to synthesize information to bring it back in the boardroom, far outnumbered the people willing to sit through another three-hour meeting.

Interestingly enough, at least four board members said, "This is the kind of contribution I was hoping to make on this board." The good news is that this new "assignment-based approach" to volunteer leadership recruitment creates a large spawning ground for people who may be interested in taking on other assignments and eventually ascending the organization to the board.

As an alternative to board service, more and more nonprofit organizations are experimenting with the idea of advisory councils or committees. For many, these bodies represent a defined way to recruit top leaders to provide coordinated input to the future as illustrated in the example of a "youth board." Advisors are tremendous knowledge philanthropy and human capital sources for discussing specific challenges that are impeding the organization from fully serving its mission.

For other nonprofits, advisory council members are viewed as ambassadors to the cause and can play a critical role for influencing policy makers, other community leaders, and top contributors.

All of these activities point to the fact that governance and its infrastructure must be viewed as a dynamic.

I highly recommend that a nonprofit board actually create, as one of its very few standing committees, an actual "Governance Committee." It is the job of this group to assure the board and the entire organization that discussions about evolving the infrastructure are taking place and the heavy lifting associated with evolving organizations is getting its due diligence. The Governance Committee also assures every board member that the tasks of governance are in check and every board meeting is both an organizational and leadership development convening.

The bottom line about governance for the nonprofit leader of the new decade is the willingness to ask some very tough questions and to make some unpopular decisions that will break hierarchical structures in order to facilitate nimble and inviting organizations.

The job begins by defining what good governance means. And, that's not an easy or short discussion.

The best starting place is agreeing on a working definition of what "policy" really means to the organization. The Third Sector gets a bad rap from the business sector because we are seen as so "process-oriented." The "cut to the chase" mentality, however, is part of what is choking our sector.

Policy, by and large, mean processes -- the framework by which the organization safeguards contributions, guarantees due diligence and assures achieving specific outcomes. With both paid and unpaid human resources at work, policies are extremely important.

Policy is the leader's greatest tool and guarantee for a cause to exercise "due diligence" in serving people and the community.

Take Succession Planning for example. The number of nonprofit organizations that have not thought through the development and tracking of a succession policy is mind boggling in an era of retiring Baby Boomers who founded a great number of nonprofit organizations in this country.

The number of nonprofits who have confused "career planning" with "succession planning" is even more alarming. Succession planning policies, like all policies, establish a pathway by which the best decisions can be made on behalf of the cause.

The nonprofit leader of the new decade must be willing to stop doing the work of the organization in the boardroom and start, as our example organization did in this section, outlining the most effective processes to guarantee that a community-based organization is, indeed, just that . . . community-based.

The policies, procedures and pathways established show that our leaders demonstrate they are excited that even more people will surround them as a result of their good thinking to value the good thinking of others.

Theory Into Practice:
The Nonprofit Leader of the New Decade

Approaching governance as a dynamic will be viewed as radical by many who have studied and taught what could be considered the rigors and discipline of governance.

What governance practices in your organization have potential to become more dynamic in their long-term benefit to the organization?

_____

_____

_____

Dynamic governance places a nonprofit board of directors "at the center" of the organization rather than "at the top" over the organization.

What are the significant leadership differences in these two very different structures?

_____

_____

_____

"Ad hoc, teams, task forces, and advisory" are more frequently occurring words of The New Decade for the nonprofit sector.

How important is it to you and to your organization to put these into practice?

_____

_____

_____

—6—

Financial Leadership In The New Decade

Financial leadership to a nonprofit begins by taking a serious poll of current levels of financial knowledge amongst its leaders, and honestly evaluating the long-term impact that has had in evolving a sustainable organization.

It doesn't seem possible that it has already been more than ten years since the phrase "Y2K" came into our business vocabulary. The excitement of the new century and all the opportunities and challenges that it represented created a flurry of predictions, promises, and cautions.

With the first decade of the new century already behind us, and, as we cross the threshold of the second, the nonprofit sector faces a radically different decade than it did ten years ago: Falling charitable contributions and eroding state funds, complex social issues facing a new generation of volunteers, and an aging workforce, complicated by an eroding allure of the Third Sector as a career which is leading to a severe talent shortage.

At the dawn of the new decade, nonprofit leaders are being confronted with economic realities, intergenerational differences and technological advances that will forever affect their infrastructures for decision-making and governance, service provision, community dialogue and voluntarism, and resource development.

In my opinion, nonprofit leadership in the new decade is going to require a deliberate reengineering of the nonprofit organization while consciously returning to some of the basic premises and practices that spawned the nonprofit movement in this country. I have some strong ideas about what that leadership approach should look like.

The essential and most basic suggestion for the "nonprofit leader in the new decade" is to significantly increase the interest in and understanding of nonprofit financial management throughout your organization.

Volunteers and staff cannot be exempt from professional development in financial management when stewardship is the responsibility of all, not some.

Unfortunately, for the vast majority of nonprofit boards of directors, the financial report during a regular convening is a staging of the "deer in the headlights" phenomena.

The nonprofit leader, in the new decade, must approach financial decision-making and financial management as a re-engineering process.

Let's start with the most basic step of all: What is the level of financial intelligence currently at play in your leadership of a nonprofit? And, what are the overall levels of financial intelligence in others who help lead?

The nonprofit leader of the new decade realizes in order to get the answers he or she is seeking it means there must be a recasting of the roles and composition of the traditional finance committee.

It also means integrating financial expertise throughout the entire infrastructure of the organization rather than segregating the financial types into a single committee. It calls for demanding pro-forma budgeting as an essential element of the strategic planning process, and maintaining a financial learning environment.

**Integrated, not segregated, financial expertise
takes a nonprofit to higher ground.**

A homogenous environment where the financial types assemble in one room and then reappear to tell the rest of us what's going on and what we should do must come to an end. The finance committee of the new decade is a diverse and balanced group of board members, senior management, outside experts and citizens.

The nonprofit finance committee meeting of the new decade assures the board that meaningful exchange of information and needed debate is taking place in committee by a diverse group of people as part of the due diligence process prior to board presentation.

An important policing role for the new finance committee is to assure that "no naked financials are allowed" in the organization, which says that every financial statement must be accompanied by a cover memorandum that explains in common, everyday language what the attached numbers mean. As a prudent form of risk management, it reaffirms that the organization's financials are not open to biased or uninformed interpretation.

Over time, the finance committee becomes viewed as the in-house, hands-on training ground for nonprofit financial management. Every nonprofit board member and every new senior manager is required to serve a term on the committee so that the overall effectiveness of the board in carrying out its fiduciary responsibilities is enhanced and management's common understanding of finance is clear.

We must stop automatically thinking that pro-bono work is what financial professionals want to do most with their volunteer time.

Nonprofit leaders of the new decade view the recruitment of a financial volunteer to serve as a mentor to a staff executive with budgeting responsibilities, is as important to the overall growth and resiliency of the organization as serving on a committee.

Strategic planning for nonprofit organizations takes on a new cachet if increased financial understanding is an objective of its leadership in the new decade. A new rule is that the strategic plan is not considered complete without a pro-forma budget. A pro-forma, or "straw budget," paints a financial picture of what the organization would look like if every aspiration were met as outlined in the plan, along with the projected costs associated with implementing the plan.

The "wish list" strategic plan simply does not cut it. Nonprofit leaders in the new decade view the strategic plan as the organization's prospectus, able to invite the financial and human capital necessary to succeed at the community service aspirations as outlined in the plan.

Moreover, the metrics developed to measure the plan will be the result of an evolved organization where diversified talents work together to recommend their own metrics rather than a group setting it for them.

My sincere hope in the new decade is for a group of leaders who take seriously the distinctions of the Third Sector from the others. Metrics and formulas developed in other sectors are no longer viewed as relevant.

Earlier this year, a group of authors published a work that looks at what they call "The Starvation Cycle" of nonprofit organizations. The genesis of the article is that the question of measuring overhead and reporting the ROI (return on investment) in corporate terms is threatening to starve our nonprofits to demise.

Admittedly, I don't have the answer. But I hope we can work together as leaders to test and find one. A nation of professionals and community leaders are anxiously waiting.

Despite all the grandiose ideas, however, we can't overlook the basics to making progress. A recent study by "BoardSource" indicates that the financials are the least understood aspect of nonprofit board leadership. In the new decade, we, as community leaders, cannot afford to let this statistic stand without jeopardizing the fates of excellent organizations that so richly contribute to our quality of life.

Theory Into Practice:
The Nonprofit Leader of the New Decade

The current level of financial knowledge and information is influencing the nonprofit's future.

What is the current level of nonprofit financial knowledge that is shaping the future of your organization and its implications?

_____

_____

Financial knowledge and its application must be viewed as an integrated activity not a segregated activity in leadership.

What are ways to integrate financial education and knowledge that benefit both the organization and its processes?

_____

_____

The Nonprofit Leader of the New Decade recognizes that creating a "check and balance" between the people who make financial recommendations and the people who approve financial recommendations is fundamental.

What is your current "check and balance" system and are there ways to enhance that organizational safeguard?

_____

_____

_____

—7—

The Nonprofit Leader As Advocate

The secret weapon for the success of the nonprofit leader of the new decade isn't all that secret. Unfortunately, it's just been treated like a secret for way too long.

Among the responses people give when asked why they are loyal to a particular nonprofit organization, is the word, "passion." A contributor who feels passionate about a particular organization is a force to reckon with.

When a loved one with a disease is being helped by an organization or hospital, the loyalty is understandably fierce and the testimony is priceless for igniting passion in others. When victims of abuse find refuge, healing, and hope, you can bet a sense of loyalty to helping others in similar situations stays with them throughout their lives.

Fueling a passion for the cause is job number one.

"How can I keep my board engaged?" "How can we raise more funds?" or, "What will keep a staff of underpaid professionals motivated to stick with their careers?" are but three examples of questions I am asked frequently.

My answer is: The Nonprofit Leader of the New Decade must understand and practice the art of advocacy if the next generation is to be motivated to get involved with and stay involved with your organization.

Many people don't know that in the good old days, the major nonprofit organizations of this nation were known as "movements:" – the YWCA movement, the Boys and Girls Club movement, and the United Way movement to name just a few.

The understanding back then was that people worked for, volunteered for, or contributed to the movement. The movement was not the organization, but what that organization stood for.

Fundraising was actually the outcome of a set of activities called "community organizing and advocacy." Organizations were deliberate about spreading the word about their cause and actively engaging people to be a part of it.

Viewing an organization as a movement is becoming a lost art. Fundraising being viewed as the result of a community organizing activity is becoming a lost science. Public engagement is being minimized to public education. And, advocacy being confused with lobbying is providing lame and unfounded excuses for leaders to stop getting into the community and organizing people to get behind their nonprofit.

Narrowly defining advocacy as lobbying is seriously jeopardizing the future of an organization.

The Internal Revenue Service has very specific guidelines about the lobbying efforts of 501/c/3 nonprofit organizations. The public agency is clear that lobbying activities are direct or grassroots activities aimed at influencing bills or resolutions, repealing proposals, referendums or similar items at the federal, state and local levels.

I can assure you that the mothers who banded together to stage The Mothers March Against Polio nearly 60 years ago weren't thinking that the disease would be eradicated by an act of Congress, Board of Supervisors, or City Council.

Likewise, the Neighborhood Watch movement is a call for people to work together and take a shared responsibility for the safety of each other, their children, and their properties. The founders of this movement weren't waiting for a decree to make people work together for the sake of safety, property values and healthy living conditions.

I would wager that your favorite cause, for example, is the result of a small group of people who shared a passion for doing something great to help others. Early on, the Founders knew the need to rally the support of more people if their dream was to succeed.

The goal – then as now – is the active engagement of people around a set of common values. The end result is the contribution of time, money, talent and loyalty.

When communities don't have people and organizations actively engaged in advancing social justice, health, safety, education and self-sufficiency, the lack of results undeniably leads to greater government involvement so that social justice, health, safety, education and self-sufficiency aren't sacrificed in society.

Throughout history, The Third Sector, through services and advocacy efforts, has been the community-based conduit for this vital work.

For those who find the recent health care reform legislation as an example of too much government, one could fairly ask the question," Where were you all these years in exploring community-based options that would develop, demonstrate and advocate for healthy citizens such that reform wasn't needed?"

**Public engagement and public education
are two different types of campaigns.**

The Nonprofit Leader of the New Decade must acknowledge that public engagement is far more important to the mission of the nonprofit than public education.

History has proven that the art of convening is the single largest contributor to the science of fundraising. Yet, the vast majority of nonprofit organizations today appear to have few leaders willing to use their valuable time to convene citizens, be in dialogue with them about their aspirations, needs and resources to make better leadership decisions.

An educated public is only one outcome of good advocacy work. The experienced nonprofit leader also knows that engagement leads to involvement which spells increased human capital and financial contributions.

If you are a part of a nonprofit whose culture is for a small group of leaders to decide on a course of action and then attempt to sell it to everybody else, you've got some hard work in front of you. The advocacy work is to support your decisions not to advocate for community decision-making. I would bet fundraising is a tough topic in your meetings.

"Why aren't people supporting our organization?" is a common question that speaks for itself when contributors don't have a chance to feel it is "their" organization. Convening, consensus building, persuasive speaking, and campaigning are the tools of advocacy that create passion and motivate financial contributions, relentless volunteers and tireless employees.

In terms of the bottom line ...
An engaged public is a contributing public.

Webster tells us that to advocate is to speak out or argue in favor of a purpose or cause. The advocate, therefore, is one who defends a cause.

I am convinced that the Nonprofit Leader of the New Decade has no choice but to consider the role that advocacy played in creating their organization and, then, will reconsider the role it must play in sustaining it.

For the leader who won't consider advocating as fundamental to their nonprofit leadership responsibilities, a wise alternative might be to consider abdicating.

Theory Into Practice:
The Nonprofit Leader of the New Decade

The misunderstanding between advocacy and lobbying will be an "Achilles' Heel" for the new decade leader.

What is a working definition of advocacy that works for you, for your organization, and for the IRS?

_____

_____

_____

We think there is a significant difference between "public engagement" and "public education" campaigns.

If you agree, what would be those significant differences?

_____

_____

_____

A fundamental tool of advocacy work is community convening. We would guess that your organization was the result of convening.

What would happen to your organization if there was a conscious decision to begin "rallying" people behind your cause?

_____

_____

_____

_____

The Epilogue:
Nonprofit of the Year

**An example of the nonprofit leader
of the new decade in the making . . .**

Imagine a competition where the competitors don't know that they are competing for an honor. Imagine an award that requires no nominations, endorsements or political maneuvering on the part of the candidates, judges or sponsors.

Each year our organization names a "Nonprofit of the Year" and it's a distinction we take very seriously. On a recent Sunday afternoon, we had the opportunity to take a local nonprofit organization by complete surprise. In front of the organization's top contributors, its board members, staff and guests, we honored the nonprofit for its achievements in the study and practice of nonprofit leadership.

Before I open up the envelope, however, it's important to look at those factors that earned a Long Beach arts organization this distinction among nonprofits throughout Southern California and Western Canada.

**Just imagine what this organization
will look like by 2020.**

The factors that go into selecting "The Nonprofit of the Year" are very simple. They represent those factors that we believe are core to "The Nonprofit Leader of the New Decade."

The first factor is refocusing the nonprofit institution into a values-driven cause. The Nonprofit of the Year decreed, after a participatory process involving its board, staff, trustees and community leaders, that it wanted to evolve from an arts organization into a leading cause of the community. Among the values approved were responsibilities for significantly contributing to the intellectual development of greater Long Beach and leading in the celebration and preservation of a uniquely American art form.

The second factor is taking a calculated risk to demonstrate the values to everyone. During a time of unprecedented cutbacks and threats to arts organizations, our award winner launched an experiment with tremendous financial and public relations risk to engage an entirely new market of enthusiasts and potential supporters. A noteworthy transformation occurred in our Nonprofit of the Year when human capital was given higher status than financial capital in long-term sustainability planning.

The third factor is a steadfast embrace of change. It's very easy for groups to speak of needing or wanting to change. The deliberate management of change, however, is anything but easy. Change can create causalities as people make difficult choices about their support or involvement in a changed organization. Change can also gobble up enormous amounts of time in emotional conflict resolution. Our Nonprofit of the Year knows these things well because of its experiences and its courage to persevere.

The fourth factor is an unwavering commitment to developing human capital. Despite limited budgets in both time and money, key board leadership at the Nonprofit of the Year each committed to more than 20 hours of professional training in board governance and fundraising over a two-year period. The organization's dynamic and driven board chair shared that leadership, emphatically stating, "It is time for the old dogs to learn some new tricks if the organization is to evolve." It played well because she made the conscious decision to lead her followers by example.

The fifth factor is a dynamic governance structure. Our award winner ran with the idea of creating a more organic approach to leadership. With goals of resiliency, objectivity, accountability and succession, a powerful governance committee has emerged that sees its job as evolving policies, practices and structures for what the organization will be rather than for what it is or as tradition has dictated. Our Nonprofit of the Year has a force to reckon with as its chair of governance demands as much vision, creativity and teamwork in the boardroom as on stage.

The sixth factor is an increased understanding and practice of savvy nonprofit financial management by all. Even in a year of scary headlines about the future viability of arts organizations, the Nonprofit of the Year closed its fiscal year with a net gain and enters the new year with working financial and human capital to invest these contributions in community outreach and broader artistic display.

As the award was presented to an unsuspecting crowd, I had the opportunity to remind everyone in the room that our community is encircled and enriched by outstanding nonprofit organizations. Each and every nonprofit in our community is contributing to the quality of life for our citizens. Every arts organization in our community is fundamental to our cultural development and diversity.

Nevertheless, as we put together our own scorecard of the six leadership factors that are taking nonprofit organizations from good to great at the dawn of the new decade, it is easy for us to look with tremendous pride at Musical Theatre West as the example for others to watch, learn from, and emulate.

Our hearty applause to Paul Garman, pictured below,

Founder and Executive Producer; Marnos Lelesi, President of the Board; and Lucy Daggett, Chair of governance, and the entire family of board leaders, management leaders, contributors and audiences.

The best news is that you have proven to all of us that in this type of competition, the real winner is our community.

Our Bottom Line:
The Nonprofit Leader of the New Decade must recognize that the bottom line of their efforts has less to do with their leadership and has everything to do with their legacy – what the next generation will inherit to continue advancing communities as a result of their leadership.

Jeffrey R. Wilcox, CFRE
The Nonprofit Leader of the New Decade

About The Author

Jeffrey R. Wilcox, CFRE, leads the largest private organization devoted to nonprofit leadership continuity in the West. Under three unique brands – Third Sector Report, Third Sector Learning, and Interim Solutions – his firm, with offices in Long Beach, CA and Vancouver, BC, provides over 140 days of leadership training each year, supports 60 affiliated and trained nonprofit executives who have served as interim professionals to over 100 nonprofits in the United States and Canada, writes The Third Sector Report for the Long Beach Business Journal and is a syndicated columnist and author.

He has over 25 years of professional nonprofit experience having held executive staff and board positions throughout the West including:
• Executive Director, Children's Hospital Foundation of Orange County
• Senior Vice-President, United Way of Greater Los Angeles
• Senior Vice-President, Valley of the Sun United Way (Phoenix)

He is a well-known teacher and authority on nonprofit management and currently serves as the Program Co-Developer and Chief Learning Officer for:
• The Board Chairs Academy
• The Wells Fargo New Executive Director's Institute of Greater Los Angeles
• The Wells Fargo Executive Leadership Institute
• The Executive Service Corps Developing Development Program
• The Executive Director's Institute of Greater Vancouver
• Next Generation Arts Leadership Project (Vancouver)
• College Bound Leadership Academy (Long Beach)

He has a resume of leading people and organizations including:
• National Trustee and National Governance Chair, Camp Fire USA (Kansas City, Missouri)
• Chairman, Conocimiento, Comprehensive Early Childhood Development – Southwest Human Development (Phoenix, Arizona)
• National Fund Distribution Redesign Committee, United Way of America (Alexandria, Virginia)
• Chapter President, Association of Fundraising Professionals (Orange County, California)
• Community Advisor, Junior Leagues of Orange County and Los Angeles

He is a contributing member of his profession as a member of Alliance for Nonprofit Management, Association of Fundraising Professionals, Association for the Research of Nonprofit Organizations and Voluntary Action, American Society for Training and Development, California Association of Nonprofits, California Society of Association Executives and International Association of Facilitators.

Acknowledgements

Special thanks to the following contributors for encouraging me and supporting me to complete "The Nonprofit Leader of the New Decade." Their words and actions illustrate the legacy of leadership to which I have advocated.

Colleen Kelly
Executive Director, Vantage Point (Vancouver)

Patrice Wong
Executive Director, Long Beach Day Nursery

Paul Garman
Executive Producer, Musical Theatre West

Dr. Elisa Nicholas
Chief Executive Officer, The Children's Clinic –Serving Children and Their Families

Maria Chavez Wilcox,
President, United Way of Orange County

Jeff Wacha, Third Sector Learning
Marilyn Neece, Third Sector Publishing
Sunny Breed

Reference:
"Good to Great and the Social Sectors: A Monograph to Accompany Good to Great" by Jim Collins. 2005

All articles contained in this
publication originally appeared in the

2599 E. 28th Street, Suite 212
Signal Hill, CA 90755-2139
562/988-1222
Web site: www.lbbj.com